Contents

KT-116-355

Cusco: The Navel of the Earth

Between 1200 CE and the early sixteenth century CE, much of South America was ruled by the great Inca empire. At the height of its power the empire was the largest nation on earth, stretching from present-day Colombia in the north to Chile in the south. The city of Cusco was the spiritual and political capital of the empire. The name 'Qosqo' means 'navel' or 'middle' in Quechua, the language of the Incas.

▲ *The ancient centre of Cusco, capital of the Inca empire, is now known as the Plaza de Armas. It is a favourite place for fiestas and strolling about in the evenings.*

Cusco stands at 3,700 m above sea-level in a deep valley in the Andes Mountains in southern Peru. The Incas developed the city in the shape of a puma, a holy symbol representing strength and power. The puma's head was on a hilltop at the temple fortress of Saqsaywaman, the stomach held the central squares and palaces and the tail was formed by the meeting point of two rivers. This pattern can still be seen today, especially from the air.

The twentieth century saw Cusco's population increase rapidly as many Peruvians migrated from the country to the city. Modern Cusco now spreads high up the surrounding hillsides and along the valley, absorbing previously small villages. However, development in the historic centre is controlled so that the city's stunning architecture is preserved. New roads have been built to keep an increasing amount of traffic moving quickly around the edge of the city.

Cusco is now a modern and vibrant city with offices, banks, cinemas, discotheques, supermarkets, sports stadiums and three universities. Yet its past is still very evident in its architecture and its rich history makes it an important tourist destination.

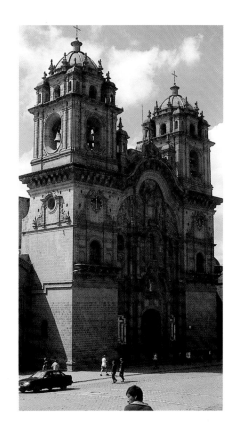

▶ *The imposing Compañia de Jesus church sits on one side of the Plaza de Armas. It is one of Cusco's many historical buildings.*

▲ *This map shows the main geographical features of Peru.*

PERU: KEY FACTS

Area: 1,285,000 sq km

Population: 28.7 million

Population density: 21 per sq km

Capital city: Lima (7.5 million)

Other major cities: Arequipa (0.75 million), Trujillo (0.65 million), Chiclayo (0.5 million),
Iquitos (0.36 million)

Highest mountain: Huascarán (6,768 m)

Longest rivers: Marañón, Ucayali (tributaries of the Amazon)

Official languages: Spanish, Quechua and Aymara

Main religion: Roman Catholic

Currency: Nuevo sol (new sol)

2 Past Times

The society of the Incas was highly organized and enormously wealthy. The legacy of this advanced civilization included beautiful cities, crop terraces, irrigation canals and a network of roads that covered over 22,000 kilometres.

In 1532 a band of Spanish *conquistadores* arrived in South America. The Spanish were captivated by the riches of the Incas, and claimed ownership of their land and wealth. They named part of their new empire Perú. The new rulers imposed their language, religion and customs and showed a complete lack of respect for the indigenous people and their culture. As a result, there were frequent revolts against Spanish rule. The most violent uprising took place in the 1780s, led by the Inca nobles Tupac Amaru and his wife Micaela Bastides. They led a victorious army against the Spanish until they were betrayed and executed with their children in Cusco.

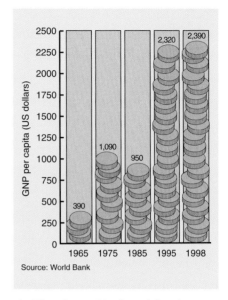

Source: World Bank

▲ *The Gross National Product of Peru has risen dramatically since 1965.*

▼ *Built upon a high mountain in central Peru, Machu Picchu is the most spectacular ruin of an Inca city. It attracts thousands of visitors from all over the world every year.*

Peru finally achieved independence from Spain in 1821 and became a democratic republic, in which the government is elected by the people. Since independence, Peru has had a range of democratic and military governments. In the early 1980s the *Sendero Luminoso* (Shining Path) movement began causing political unrest and economic insecurity through acts of terrorism that aimed to overthrow the government and create a socialist state. Partly as a result, President Alberto Fujimori changed the constitution and established a more autocratic system of government.

Between 1990 and 2000, Fujimori increased his control over judicial and democratic systems and limited Peruvians' personal freedoms. In 2000, Fujimori and many of his colleagues were exposed as corrupt, and the president fled to Japan in disgrace. Peru has now returned to democratic government with wide international support.

▶ *Modern office buildings in Lima, known as the 'city of kings' by the Spaniards.*

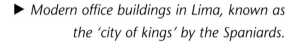

IN THEIR OWN WORDS

'My name is Wilfredo Loayza. I'm 66 years old and have three children. The best thing about Peru at the moment is that after a period with a very corrupt government we now have a new democracy. We hope that things will get better both for families and the country as a whole. For the future, I think it is only if the next generation has a good education that we will be able to change people's outlook.

'The past is still present in today's Peru in the countryside, where the same sort of agriculture is practised as it was in the time of the Incas. *Campesinos* (peasant farmers) use the ancient terraces and irrigation systems. In the mountains and rainforest, the majority of ordinary people still follow the same ancestral customs they had before the Spanish conquest. They believe in their gods and Apus, the spirits of the mountains. Culture has changed most in the cities.'

3

Landscape and Climate

Peru lies south of the equator, on the Pacific coast of South America. It is the third largest country in South America, after Brazil and Argentina. It has three distinct regions that run parallel to each other from north to south.

Coast

Peru's coastal region is a narrow desert strip running the length of the country between the Pacific Ocean and the Andes Mountains. Although the landscape is generally dry and flat, there are also a number of fertile valleys in this area. The rivers running through these valleys begin in the mountains and flow towards the Pacific Ocean. Annual average temperatures range from 18 to 24 °C, with the hottest period in the December to March summer season.

▲ Peru has an extensive coastline. Riding the waves and sunbathing on the beach are favourite pastimes for people who live near the sea.

Mountains

The Andes is the longest chain of mountains in the world. In Peru, it forms three irregular ranges, running from the north to the south of the country. At over 6,700 m, Huascarán is the highest mountain in the country.

▶ The Andes is the second highest mountain chain on earth. The high peaks and low valleys of the Andes are one reason for Peru's varied climates and landscape.

The mountain region has five distinct climatic zones. These range from warm, where temperatures often reach 27 °C by day, to glacial, where temperatures can stay below zero degrees all year round.

Rainforest

More than half of Peru is covered in forest. To the east of the mountain ranges, cloud forests slope gently towards the Amazonian rainforest. The forest here has a humid, wet and tropical climate with temperatures ranging between 22 and 36 °C.

At lower altitudes temperatures are higher throughout the year, reaching a maximum of 41 °C. Rainfall is often heavy, and accompanied by violent storms. Many species of insects, birds, animals and reptiles flourish in the rainforest, and over six hundred different types of fish swim in the rainforest rivers.

▲ *The Amazon rainforest has always been an important resource, providing firewood and building materials for local people.*

IN THEIR OWN WORDS

'I'm Roberto Tamani. I live in Nuevo Luz de Fatima, a village on Lake Yarinacocha in the rainforest near Pucallpa. I have three children, all boys. I have a small plot of land where I grow yucca (a root crop, also called cassava) and maize for my family, and watermelons to sell.

'I have to go fishing as well as do farming but we only catch small fish like piranhas (which have a lot of bones), catfish and sardines. I don't know if my sons will stay here. When they have families there won't be enough land for each to grow their own food. The population has grown but the amount of land has stayed the same.'

Climate change

Like many countries throughout the world, Peru is beginning to feel the effects of climate change. Air pollution is causing severe damage to the earth's ozone layer, which has in turn resulted in a rise in global temperatures. Many factors are affecting the climate of Peru, including industrial pollution and deforestation in the Amazon. Deforestation can cause a change in rainfall patterns and also results in soil erosion. The most noticeable recent change in Peru's climatic conditions is the recurrence of El Niño episodes, which have had a severe impact on Peru's natural environment and its people.

▲ Deforestation and heavy rain lead to serious soil erosion in parts of Peru.

El Niño

El Niño ('The Child') came by its name because it often occurs at Christmas, and baby Jesus is sometimes referred to as 'The Child'. El Niño is a natural effect that reverses the normal temperature and current patterns in the southern Pacific Ocean.

◀ Despite torrential rain it's business as usual in this colourful market in Pisaq in southern Peru. Such downpours become more frequent during El Niño episodes.

IN THEIR OWN WORDS

'My name is Lucilla Gamboa Lopez. I used to live in the small village of Santa María in La Convención province (in the southern sierra). On 27th February 1998 I lost everything.

'It was 1 a.m. and everyone was sleeping. The train conductor came to the house and shouted at us to run as fast as we could because the river water was rising very quickly. My five sisters, my sister-in-law and I fled. We had no clothes, nothing. In the night we saw the river eat up our land – we kept having to move up higher and higher. The rain was so heavy we had nowhere to shelter. We were four days in the mountains without eating or drinking. Helicopters were looking for people but no one saw us.

'More than eighty people died and our whole community disappeared. We had to come to Cusco because we'd lost our farm – 500 turkeys and 480 guinea pigs were drowned. Our coffee was ready for harvesting – that disappeared along with all our fruit trees. Now we are living with relatives.'

During El Niño a change in the usual east-west wind patterns in the Pacific Ocean causes an increase in sea surface temperatures. This in turn creates low air pressure, which results in heavy rainfall over Peru and neighbouring countries.

Floods and landslides along Peru's coast and inland regions occur frequently during El Niño episodes. These have caused much destruction and loss of life during recent times, as in 1982-1983, 1992-1993 and 1997-1998. Unfortunately, El Niño episodes are becoming more frequent and more intense.

▶ *Landslides are very frequent during the rainy season, especially during El Niño episodes.*

4

Natural Resources

Agriculture

The varying climates in different regions of Peru make possible the cultivation of many different crops. Vegetables, root crops, pulses and fruit range from well-known varieties to exotic species little known outside Peru, such as olluco (a yellow-orange root crop) and pacay (a long sweet fruit). Many Andean crops, such as potatoes, have been cultivated since ancient times. There are more than 200 potato varieties well suited to Peru's high altitudes.

Today, the major areas of agricultural production are in Arequipa, Majes, Tumbes, Piura and the central coastal area, where rivers have been dammed to create oases where cotton, rice, grapes and wheat are grown. There are plans to dam some of the larger rivers in the rainforest in order to expand the production of rice and other products suitable for the altitude and climate of the area.

Trade with other countries has increased rapidly over the last twenty years. Peru now exports vegetables to Bolivia, maize to Japan and coffee and tropical fruits to Europe and

▲ *Harvesting cassava by hand on a small plot of land in the rainforest.*

▼ *Here two different types of potatoes grow alongside corn. The hill in the background is being reforested.*

North America. Tea, cocoa, sugar-cane, tobacco and grapes are also produced for national use and export. The pattern of exports is changing, as in the past most goods were channelled through Lima. Now, much produce goes directly from regional companies and co-operatives.

Minerals

Peru has large deposits of zinc, phosphates, copper, mercury, gold, iron and silver. The biggest mining centres are at Cerro del Pasco in the central Andes, Toquepala in the southern Andes and Marcona on the south coast. Gold is mined mainly in the Amazon basin. Peru is the world's second biggest exporter of bismuth, third of silver and seventh of copper. Peru exports 90 per cent of the copper it mines.

▶ *Fertilizers for agriculture and explosives for mining are both manufactured in this factory.*

IN THEIR OWN WORDS

'I'm Fernando Solis Gutierrez. I'm a mining engineer at the Cachimayo sodium nitrate factory. We make two products: explosives for the mines, and fertilizers. The explosive we make is like dynamite but much stronger and much cheaper. In the past, miners just stuck sticks of dynamite in the rock and hoped for the best. Our explosive is more accurate. The process of mining hasn't really changed, but the technology that enables us to process the minerals is now more effective.'

Energy sources

Over 80 per cent of Peru's energy requirement is produced by hydroelectric power. There are power plants near Lima, in Machu Picchu and Apurimac in the southern sierra and in Cerro del Pasco in the central sierra. There are also plans to expand the number of hydroelectric plants, especially in the Huallaga valley in the central sierra.

Petrol for transport, cooking and the production of plastics is extracted from oil rigs in the ocean and, increasingly, from the Amazon basin. Two pipelines now connect oil wells deep inland with a refinery on the north coast at Talara. There are other inland refineries at Pucallpa and Iquitos.

Recently, the government has begun work on the Camisea natural gas project to produce gas for domestic and commercial use. This will make piped gas available to many homes for the first time. Solar energy is also being explored on a much smaller scale.

▼ *A hydroelectric dam near Machu Picchu. Hydroelectricity is a major source of energy all over Peru.*

Forestry

Peru's forests are an important fuel source for use in cooking and heating. Forest plants are also used for medicinal purposes.

The global demand for Amazonian timber has resulted in intensive and uncontrolled timber logging in many of Peru's natural woodlands and rainforest. Species of trees such as ishpingo, caoba (mahogany), aguano and cedro (cedarwood) and rare trees like pashaco and capirona are especially popular because of their beautiful finish for furniture and flooring. However, they take many years to grow and it can also take a long time to restore the ecosystems destroyed by logging. The economic benefits of extensive logging are therefore short-term, and Peru's natural environment may suffer permanent damage.

▶ *In some areas of the mountains and rainforest, wood is the only available source of fuel for cooking and heating.*

IN THEIR OWN WORDS

'I'm Telita Mendes. I'm thirteen. My family and I make bracelets and necklaces from jungle seeds and piranha and crocodile teeth and hope there is someone to sell them to. Sometimes tourists come and visit us here. We are very pleased when they buy something. We need money to buy soap, salt, sugar and kerosene. Everything else comes from our *chacra* (plot of land).

'The forest is changing. The big trees are disappearing. Downriver they have electricity. There are these lights for the street that stay on all night so they can read and make necklaces – but all the insects come too. They have a road, but it's very bumpy and muddy. It's nicer to travel on the river.'

Oceans

Peru's ocean is a rich source of fish because the cold Humboldt current offshore provides a good environment for plankton, which fish feed on. Anchovies and pilchards are caught by fishing fleets that have refrigeration equipment onboard. These are landed in coastal ports such as Chimbote, which has a number of canning factories. Peruvian tinned fish is exported to Europe.

▲ *Like many fishermen in Peru, these men still use a small fishing boat.*

Fishmeal, a fertilizer and livestock feed produced from fish and fish parts, has traditionally been one of Peru's biggest exports. However, in 2001 the European Union stopped the importing of fishmeal to EU countries. The measure formed part of a series of actions taken to prevent the spread of BSE (bovine spongiform encephalopathy) in cows. Peru's fishmeal industry has shrunk dramatically as a result.

IN THEIR OWN WORDS

'My name is Pedro Luís Baldo. I am 54 years old. I have six children and live in Chorillos, Lima. I've been a fisherman for forty years and things have changed a lot in that time. Now there are hardly any fish left. I go out for three or four hours and just come back with a small bucket of rey, lorna, lisa, cabisa – all small fish. My boat is just a rowing boat so I can't go out very far. Offshore you get the Japanese factory boats, which don't come into the port. They freeze their catch onboard. Up the coast there are larger boats that catch tuna and anchovies for the canneries.'

There is now a risk of over fishing in the Pacific, especially as fleets from countries such as Japan have been entering Peru's territorial waters. El Niño has also seriously affected catches because it causes sea temperatures to rise. This results in a lack of oxygen in the water and kills off plankton supplies. Anchovy production dropped by 33 per cent during 2001. To diversify the fishing industry, shrimp and lobster farms are being developed in mangrove areas on Peru's north coast.

Lakes and rivers

Fish supplies from Peru's lakes and rivers are plentiful. Lake Titicaca is the highest lake in the world to have fishing fleets, which are based in the port of Puno. Amazonian fish such as paiche (a large white fish) are widely traded within Peru, reaching markets in the mountains. Farming of freshwater fish such as trout is increasing in parts of the Andes.

▼ *Fish from Peru's oceans, lakes and rivers are all sold at this market stall.*

5

The Changing Environment

Effects of urbanization

Over the past sixty years vast numbers of Peruvians have moved from rural areas to urban centres in an attempt to escape poverty, land shortage or terrorism. Today over 70 per cent of the population lives in towns and cities, compared to about 35 per cent in 1940. This change has had a dramatic impact on Peru's urban environment.

Pollution

The rapid increase in the urban population has caused major problems of pollution. The air is most polluted along the coast, where there are many cities and factories. Almost a third of Peru's population lives in Lima, the most populated and most polluted urban area in the country. The lack of rainfall in the desert area around Lima, together with a growing number of cars and factories, causes a thick smog that has serious effects on people's health.

Peru's cities also have problems with waste disposal. Increased use of plastic and paper packaging for food and household goods has led to rubbish piling up in streets and on wasteland.

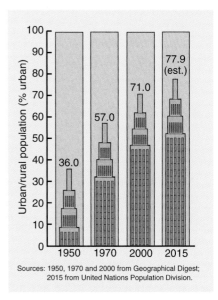

Sources: 1950, 1970 and 2000 from Geographical Digest; 2015 from United Nations Population Division.

▲ *The percentage of the Peruvian population living in cities almost doubled between 1950 and 2000. This trend is expected to continue.*

◄ *A new township under construction on the edge of Lima. Many people who move from rural areas to the cities have to live in poor-quality housing.*

Although pollution isn't as serious in rural areas, the rapid growth of towns and villages has led to rubbish and sewage being dumped in rivers. Pesticide use is also increasingly contaminating soil and water in the countryside.

Tackling environmental problems

The severity of these environmental problems has led to the development of an environmental movement in Peru. A national ecology political party has been founded, and the government is introducing measures to protect the environment. Nationally, drivers are encouraged to use cleaner, lead-free petrol. Many schools have recycling bins for different kinds of waste and pupils learn about various types of pollution in science classes.

▲ *Both the air and coastal waters of Lima are seriously polluted.*

IN THEIR OWN WORDS

'I'm Marleny Huamani Chacón. I'd like to live in the country because the air is cleaner but it's impossible; here it's hard to get a job, but in the countryside it's even harder. In the last few years the number of cars has grown a lot and this is causing a lot of pollution. Recycling would help the town – the plastic bottles and bags need to be dealt with; they don't decompose so they cause litter. At the moment nothing is being done to control pollution. We need to control the number of cars and the exhaust fumes from buses, which give us sore throats. When my grandparents were young there were no cars and everyone walked everywhere.

'In the centre of town there's not much of a water problem because there is a lake, but in the suburbs we only get water for half a day. If there is no water at all in the taps we take water from the river and use purifying tablets.'

Deforestation

During the 1960s, the military government introduced a policy of land clearance in the Andes and the Amazon to create more agricultural land. People were encouraged to clear the land by burning small areas of forest. This frequently led to larger fires that burned out of control for weeks.

Widespread deforestation has created soil erosion in many areas. This becomes especially serious during the rainy seasons (spring and summer) or during El Niño episodes, when heavy rain causes landslides. In order to limit this type of environmental damage, the government has created conservation parks in five different parts of Peru. These are special reserves in which all logging and clearance of land is prohibited. The Forestry Commission and special police ensure that the conservation parks are maintained and new controls enforced.

▼ *A sawmill in Pucallpa. Every year, hundreds of thousands of rainforest trees are cut down to be used in furniture and flooring.*

Reforestation

In recent years successive governments of Peru have made a policy of reforestation in areas most affected by loss of trees. In 1990, over 9,000 hectares of land had been reforested and by 1997 the annual figure had reached 100,000 hectares. Peru won a prestigious World Bank prize in 2002 for a reforestation project in the Amazon basin.

Restoration of woodland benefits local people in many ways. As well as improving air quality, trees can be selectively cut down and re-planted, providing an ongoing source of income through the sale of timber.

▶ *Some of the many Peruvians involved in planting tree seedlings for reforestation.*

IN THEIR OWN WORDS

'My name is Raúl Pozo. I spent 25 years working in the forestry department. In the 1960s large-scale reforestation began in the regions of Cusco, Cajamarca and Huancayo. This was necessary because a lot of mountains had lost their vegetation. We planted thousands of hectares of eucalyptus trees in *campesino* communities to teach farmers to avoid soil erosion and give them a resource – wood – which they could use in many different ways. We planted some fruit trees that provide a microclimate and benefit agricultural production. Now nearly all communities have woods and rely on them. If the communities only grow potatoes they don't earn much and will always be poor. With a forest they can earn thousands of *soles* through selling the wood. Then they have the power to buy a truck or tractor. The benefits occur in ten to fifteen years time with the growth of trees.'

6

The Changing Population

Over the past decades Peru's population has been growing steadily, at a rate of about 1.5 per cent per year. Life expectancy is 71 years for women and 66 years for men, which is just under the average for Latin America and the Caribbean. Child mortality – the rate of deaths of under five year olds – has dropped steadily, from 75 deaths per thousand births in 1990 to 52 in 2000. The average number of children per family is about three, and this figure is continuing to decrease. In the past Peruvian women often had five or more children.

Increasing mobility

The valleys and peaks of the Andes and the extent of tropical rainforest in the Amazon basin used to make it difficult to travel around Peru. This meant that rural people lived largely within their own communities, producing their food and other goods they needed. However, recent government policy has been to strengthen transport networks. Peru is now served by over 130 airstrips and over 70,000 kilometres of roads. This has resulted in a more mobile population and people from a range of different backgrounds living in both urban and rural centres.

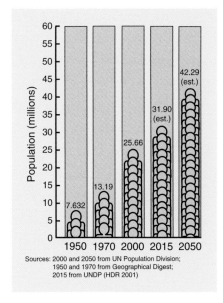

Sources: 2000 and 2050 from UN Population Division; 1950 and 1970 from Geographical Digest; 2015 from UNDP (HDR 2001)

▲ As in many developing countries, Peru's population has increased dramatically since 1950.

◄ Peruvian families watch a football game together. The children will probably live longer than their parents and have smaller families.

IN THEIR OWN WORDS

'I'm Marcelina. I was born in a small village near Puno. I decided to come to Lima as I can earn more here. I have a job cooking and cleaning for a family. In Lima there are people who lack for nothing and others who have nothing. I like the parks here and in the city you can learn a lot. In the country there's nothing, no television – we didn't even have a radio, so you know nothing of what is happening in the world. If I had stayed in the countryside my life would be very different – I'd just be working on our bit of land and looking after the animals. Life is happy and you live simply, but because no one has anything, no one can help you if you need money. I'm going to stay in the city now.'

Population distribution

In 1940, 62 per cent of Peru's population lived in mountain regions. By 1990 this had dropped to 36 per cent. During the same period, the proportion of Peruvians living in coastal areas grew from 25 per cent to 53 per cent. In contrast, the number of people living in the rainforest has stayed almost constant, dropping from 13 per cent in 1940 to 11 per cent in 1990.

▼ *A road winds across a plateau near Abancay in the Andes. Areas such as these are becoming more easily accessible with surfaced roads.*

Return to the countryside

One of the main causes for the rapid growth of cities was terrorism in rural areas. The capture of key leaders of terrorist networks during the early 1990s and the more recent return to democracy means that terrorism is no longer a major threat in Peru. As a result, some people are deciding to return to country life. Government projects have encouraged urban residents to move out of the cities and seek new lives in the sierra and *selva*. Many professional Limeños (people who live in Lima) are moving to regional towns and cities such as Huancayo and Cusco, where they hope to have a better quality of life than in the overcrowded capital.

A varied population

Peru is a racially diverse country. Over half of Peruvians are described as 'indigenous Indian' and nearly a third as *mestizo* (mixed race). *Mestizos* include descendants of African,

▲ *The crowded conditions in most Peruvian cities make the possibility of moving to the countryside an attractive option for many urban residents.*

Chinese and Japanese immigrants, as well as white Europeans. The recent arrival of large numbers of people from the mountains in major cities has at times resulted in social tensions, and there have been incidents of racism. However, because Peru has had a multicultural population for centuries, it is generally a tolerant and inclusive society.

In recent years Peruvians have become increasingly proud of their ancestry. One reason for this is the growing interest in documentary-making and publishing about the Inca culture and Peru's history. A greater understanding of Peru's past is slowly leading to greater acceptance of indigenous people in urban areas.

▲ *Peruvians from different ethnic backgrounds working together in Lima.*

IN THEIR OWN WORDS

'My name is Maria Montalban de Olivares. I am the manager of this coffee shop. I've experienced very little racism myself, but perhaps because I have a nice job and my friends are educated I am respected in the community. Racism does occur in Peru – especially in the big cities like Lima and Arequipa. I lived in Arequipa for four years and nothing bad happened to me but I saw it happening to others. My children are mixed race – my husband is *Criollo*, part *Quechua* and part Spanish. My daughter is quite dark but hasn't had any problems at school. I have no idea of my roots. I suppose my ancestors were brought from Africa to pick cotton, unless they came with Pizarro, the *conquistador*.'

7

Changes at Home

Family life

Family life is very important in Peru. Children often live in extended families, in which everyone accepts their specific chores and responsibilities. Aunts and uncles, grandparents and cousins may live together in a single home. Friends are also closely involved in family life, often becoming informal foster parents to children.

However, family life in Peru is changing. Young people are trying to become self-reliant by looking for paid work and living outside the home at an earlier age than in the past. Children used to grow up with a strong sense of responsibility towards their parents and took care of them in old age. Although this tradition remains strong in the Andes and rainforest areas, in urban centres young people are seeking increasing independence from their families. In the past older siblings often took full responsibility for running the household, but today many young people want to take advantage of new opportunities for work and education.

▲ This family live in Lake Yarinacocha, in the rainforest. Most families here maintain a traditional way of life.

▼ In Peruvian families, everyone is expected to share responsibilities. This family is working together to prepare flour from cassava roots.

IN THEIR OWN WORDS

'I'm Pamela Zirm Ruiz. I'm fifteen. I spend a lot of time in the home helping. I do all the daily chores with my mum, washing dishes, cleaning and cooking. I'm responsible for the chickens. We have twenty of them. I have to feed them and collect the eggs. I've given them all names – the problem is that I don't like seeing my friends in the soup!

'My life is very different to my grandmother's. She had to work from a very young age. She didn't go to school but worked sowing plants to sell and working in the home. Now I've finished school and want to go to university.'

Marriage

The importance of the Catholic religion in Peru means that most couples marry in a church ceremony. Intermarriage between different ethnic groups and economic classes is common.

Most young Peruvians are choosing to marry later than their parents did. Until the late twentieth century, it was very common for women to marry and have a family in their late teens. Today, many women wait until their late twenties or early thirties to marry. This is partly because of the increasing opportunities for women to take part in higher education and establish their own careers.

▶ *The wedding of a Peruvian Chinese couple in Lima. Like most Peruvians, they have chosen to have a traditional Catholic ceremony.*

Religion

Although the number of Peruvians regularly attending mass is falling, most Peruvians still consider themselves Catholic. Peruvian Catholicism is heavily influenced by traditional Andean spirituality. Traditional ceremonies such as *Cortapelo* – a hair cutting to mark the end of babyhood – are widely practised.

During the 1960s and 70s, Popes John XXIII and Paul VI encouraged the Church to be more open to change. Radical priests campaigned against human rights abuses and political repression. In more recent times there has been growing discontent about the rituals of Catholic worship, requests for donations and an increase in foreign priests who don't speak local languages or understand local culture.

Meanwhile, membership of relatively new churches such as the Evangelists and Jehovah's Witnesses is rising in Peru. Some of these new churches attract worshippers by offering free health care or other incentives.

▲ *This girl is taking a doll of the baby Jesus to church at Ephiphany to be blessed.*

Tackling poverty

Over a quarter of Peruvians live in extreme poverty, and overcoming inequalities amongst the population is one of the country's biggest challenges. While many Peruvians, especially in urban areas, have a high standard of living, others live in basic housing and often do not have enough food to eat. In poorer areas, people organize communal kitchens to make sure that everyone eats healthy meals. The indigenous communities of Peru generally have less access to education and health care than other sections of the population.

IN THEIR OWN WORDS

'My name is Miguel Chavez Ramírez. When I was young I left Peru to look for work. I trained as a pilot and an economist and I was working in Europe, but then I heard about the United Nations Convention that gives rights to indigenous people with respect to their education and traditions. I visited Peru and saw that people didn't know their rights so I decided to come back and work on this.'

Foreign aid programmes, in which wealthier countries provide Peru with money, health care or food, are helping some Peruvians overcome poverty. Many middle-class Peruvians also work with poorer communities to improve their lives and educate them about their rights.

▼ *An example of an urban community organizing a self-help scheme: a soup kitchen in San Juan de Lurigancho.*

◀ *The many tropical fruits that grow in Peru produce delicious juices. Fresh fruit is now more widely available than ever before and so too are Western-style soft drinks.*

Diet

The improvements in road, rail and air transport have had a major impact on the Peruvian diet. More fresh food, including fish, vegetables and fruit is available and pasteurized milk and cheeses now reach the majority of the population. However, different regions remain strongly influenced by what food is readily available. Every area has special dishes, such as chiriuchu in the Andes, which is made from different meats including guinea pig.

In Peru's urban centres a wide variety of international food is now available, including Western-style fast foods such as pizzas and burgers. A positive change in the Peruvian diet is that meals are generally better balanced, with less red meat and more pulses and native cereals.

▶ *One of Peru's many fast food restaurants. These are particularly appealing to people who work long hours and don't have time to cook for themselves.*

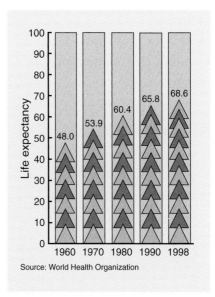

The importance of a healthy diet is being taught widely in schools and this is one reason behind the nation's improving health.

Health and medicine

Between 1992 and 2000 over thirty new hospitals and 900 clinics were built in Peru. There has also been a rise in the number of trained doctors and health workers, particularly in rural areas. The state health insurance system provides health care for an annual fee and government employees receive free health care. Peruvians who do not join the state scheme can pay for consultations at hospitals or private practices.

Today many Peruvians use both Western medicine and traditional remedies. Some plants are used widely to cure simple illnesses such as colds, stomach upsets or fevers. Many healers still practise Andean mysticism, linking spiritual and physical healing with a detailed knowledge of healing plants.

Life expectancy chart:

Year	Life expectancy
1960	48.0
1970	53.9
1980	60.4
1990	65.8
1998	68.6

Source: World Health Organization

▲ *An improving health care system is partly responsible for the increase in the life expectancy of Peruvians.*

IN THEIR OWN WORDS

'I am known as El Condor. I live in Huasao, a village of shamans a 40-minute bus ride from Cusco. My work is about getting people to value their spiritual as well as their physical side. This is how my work differs from Western medicine. Patients come when they are sick or have to make difficult decisions and I help them. My work isn't just about the material world – many people are too concerned with money and success. I help people cleanse their bodies and their minds. My work is about communicating with the gods of the mountains – the Apus – and asking them to help people.

'Many people come to see me. They recognize the powers I have and think I can help them when the other doctors can't. I charge the same amount – ten dollars – for a consultation. I learned from a master and every year I pass on my gifts to two or three new healers. With the stress and problems of life today people need us traditional healers more than ever.'

Education

Although state education in Peru is free for every child, parents have to pay for materials, uniforms and examination fees. Children start school at age six and finish at age sixteen. During the 1990s many private fee-paying schools were established, especially in coastal areas. Then two different strands of secondary education were introduced. Fourteen-year-olds can choose to pursue academic studies at a *bachillerato* or attend a technical college. Most Peruvian children attend primary school, 70 per cent go on to secondary school and over 30 per cent of Peruvians undertake higher education.

▲ These children on an island in Lake Titicaca often have their lessons outside.

University education is free in Peru, except for the registration fees and entrance examinations. The growing demand for higher education has caused the creation of many private universities. Peruvians value education highly, and poor families struggle to help their children gain a degree. A very popular saying in Peru is 'there is no better inheritance for children than that of a good education.'

◀ Plenty to read about. A city news stand displays all the latest magazines.

Communications

Until the 1980s there were many areas of Peru that had no electricity and the main medium of communication was radio. The spread of education means that today 90 per cent of Peruvians can read and write, and local and national newspapers are flourishing. Television and telephone ownership is increasing rapidly. In some rural areas where few people own televisions, a bar or restaurant that has a television set is the focal point for the whole community.

This revolution in communications has had many benefits. Peruvians are more aware of the world around them and of their rights and responsibilities. However, some people believe that television is partly responsible for the weakening of traditional values. Others feel that watching television decreases communication and understanding within the family.

▲ *Dreaming of what to buy. This shop offers a wide range of electronic equipment. Unfortunately, many Peruvians cannot afford adequate housing, let alone high-tech goods.*

IN THEIR OWN WORDS

'My name is Ana. I'm 34. I worked for eighteen months in TV as a reporter but now I've given it up to work with *campesinos* using video and radio to produce teaching materials for them. My personal opinion is that television destroys communication in the family. My mother didn't have television so she had time to develop other interests. Her mind was open. She had no stress and was very calm. Her family communicated with each other much better. In the past children had very natural games and made their own toys. Now TV influences us a lot. There's a lot of violence on TV and children learn to be violent from it. TV is here, we can't do without it but we need to control it. I know a family who don't have a TV and the children write, they play the piano, they are much more creative.'

Leisure

Traditional children's games in Peru include *chapa-chapa* (hide and seek), *matagente* (piggy in the middle) and *tiros* (marbles). In recent years, electronic games and television viewing have become very popular with children, which means they play together less often. The increasing amount of traffic in cities also makes street games dangerous and consequently children spend more time indoors.

Cinemas and discos are favourite pastimes of Peruvian teenagers. Travel and internal tourism have become more common with the opening of new roads linking areas that were previously difficult to reach. *Paseos* – outings made by families to the countryside – are still widely enjoyed. Meanwhile, blood sports such as cock fighting are dying out across Peru, although the bullring in Lima still stages occasional bull-fighting spectacles.

▲ *A young Peruvian with time to spare enjoys an electronic game.*

◀ *These children in the Amazon entertain themselves with a game of volleyball, which is popular throughout Peru.*

IN THEIR OWN WORDS

'I'm Eduardo Sullca. Football is what I like best. It's our national game, although some people play volleyball and basketball. We have footballers who go abroad to play with international teams. You earn masses more abroad. Unfortunately there are lots of good teams in Latin America so we don't always make it to the World Cup. We practise wherever we can, like me, just by the side of the road.'

Sport

As health education has improved, sport has become more important to Peruvians. Favourite sports include cycling, aerobics and gymnastics. Volleyball is also very popular, particularly since the Peruvian women's team won an Olympic medal in 1988. The government encourages physical education in schools for all ages at least twice a week and there are many local and regional sporting events.

Football is Peru's national passion. Children are coached from an early age and in recent years girls have started playing and acting as referees. There is a strong national league and the entire country celebrates when Peru qualifies for the World Cup.

▶ *Wealthy Peruvians enjoy adventure sports such as hang-gliding.*

8

Changes at Work

In the past, many young Peruvians followed their parents into agricultural, mining or factory work. With more young people gaining university-level qualifications, the workforce is now becoming more skilled.

Private enterprise

Major political changes in Peru have led to changing work opportunities. Large state companies such as Petrogas have been taken over by private enterprise. Private foreign investment in communications, railways and other service and tourism industries has created more jobs for skilled workers. Furthermore, many of these companies have training schemes for unskilled workers. Private investment is also creating new opportunities in banking, supermarkets and telecommunications.

◀ A travel agent in a busy Lima office. Peru's service sector is expanding rapidly.

Food exports

In the past, manufacturing and food processing industries used to be primarily along Peru's coast, with very little manufacturing taking place in the Andes and rainforest region.

Production in these areas was mostly for local consumption or use, such as barley for local breweries.

However, improved transport links with mountain and forest locations have opened up opportunities to process and export organic food products. In the rainforest, co-operatives are introducing new products such as pure fruit juices to the national market. In the Andes, native cereal crops such as quinoa, mixed with fruit, nuts and honey make excellent muesli, cereal mixes and energy bars.

The development of food industries in rural areas is creating job opportunities for local people who have previously relied on subsistence agriculture, or, more recently, tourism for their income.

▲ *Measuring processed quinoa to be packed and transported for the local and national markets. Food processing is a new industry in the sierra.*

IN THEIR OWN WORDS

'I'm Viviana Vargas Concha. I am 27. I have worked at Inca Sur for the last two years. Our company, which is thirty years old, turns traditional Andean organic produce – cocoa, quinoa, kiwicha (a small grain) and broad beans – into food products. The cocoa is made into organic chocolate, the broad beans are turned into cream soup, the quinoa into flour. At the moment we are working with maca (a native root crop) which is very high in vitamins and proteins and good for combating stress. Our main product, kiwigen, we export to Colombia and Mexico (kiwigen is a processed form of kiwicha). Those are our only foreign markets at the moment although we are expecting to expand. Our business helps the economy because we give jobs to thirty workers in Cusco and ninety in Lima. We are trying to grow food the way the Incas did with natural fertilizers. It's much healthier than using a lot of chemicals.'

Farming

Over the last decades of the twentieth century the agricultural industry on Peru's coast became increasingly mechanized. In accessible regions of the Andes, the workforce is now aided by machinery, especially in larger co-operatives and land holdings. However, in most parts of Peru farm work is carried out mainly by hand with the help of animal-drawn ploughs. *Ayni* – an ancient custom of sharing work – is still strong in some urban and most rural areas, especially in the Andes and rainforest where large groups of people come together to work collectively on planting and harvesting.

Women at work

Traditionally, skilled and educated women worked as secretaries, nurses and school teachers. Nowadays, women work in engineering, management, banking, the law, medicine, tourism and politics. Women are still paid less than men for the same work and are frequently overlooked for promotion in favour of men. Many women join trade unions that help them tackle these obstacles. The government has recently created a Ministry for Women's and Children's Affairs that aims to address problems such as sexual inequality.

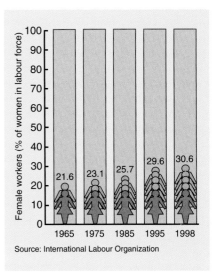

Source: International Labour Organization

▲ *The number of Peruvian women who work outside the home is increasing slowly but surely.*

◀ *More and more women are filling positions in traditionally male fields. Here a forestry engineer inspects tree seedlings.*

In the past, young women from poorer families often found work in wealthier households. While this is still common, the development of private enterprise means that there is now a much wider range of positions available to unskilled workers in areas such as retailing or manufacturing.

In rural areas women work on the land and run small businesses based on products such as weaving and craftwork. They often organize co-operatives so that they can pool their resources and profits.

▲ *Peru's retail sector provides a growing number of jobs for unskilled young women.*

IN THEIR OWN WORDS

'I am Karoll Borda and I'm 21. I'm studying information technology, in particular systems analysis. I'm in my third and last year of studies. I'm taking these courses because I see this as a good career move for the future. Now women are going for the same jobs as men – they are just as capable of doing everything. There are those who want to keep women in the home and not let them develop but they are the old fashioned ones. Both the government and women's organizations have been encouraging women to develop. In my class there are twenty women and twenty-eight men so we are catching up.'

Tourism

The increase in tourist arrivals from all around the world has opened many new employment opportunities for Peruvians. In recent years international tourists have been demanding a growing variety of tourism options. These include eco-tours, study tours and rainforest tours, all of which require staff with specialist skills and knowledge. The number of higher education courses in hospitality and tourism is constantly increasing in an effort to deal with this demand.

In many parts of the Peruvian Amazon, indigenous people who for centuries have been almost completely isolated from the outside world are now visited by people from many different countries. In such places local clothes, customs and dances are becoming sights for tourists to photograph and admire. While there are some concerns that the lives of indigenous people are being exploited, tourism does provide these communities with a valuable source of income.

▲ *Every year thousands of tourists come to Peru to visit Machu Picchu, one of South America's most important archaeological sites.*

◄ *Visitors to Peru on an eco-tour. The growing interest in eco-tourism means that there is an increasing demand for nature experts and specialist tour guides in Peru.*

IN THEIR OWN WORDS

'I am Raúl Ramírez. I have a degree in tourism and now I'm studying natural history by myself because I work with naturalists doing specialist tours. I like my work because I meet new people and I learn about other societies and cultures. I'm teaching my clients about the cultural heritage and environment of my country, and they tell me about theirs.

'Some Americans don't want to take risks; they don't consider South America a secure place. We have to look to other markets – Europe and Australia, and now also more people from Asia are coming – from China, Korea and Japan. There are good and bad things about tourism. It's good because it helps the local economy but bad because it increases prices for local people. Also when places are over-visited they lose what made them special in the first place.'

Although Peru's tourist industry is growing steadily and working in tourism can be highly profitable, natural disasters or terrorist incidents can mean an instant and dramatic drop in tourist numbers. Every downturn in tourism causes economic hardship for local working people, from businesses, shops and transport to guides, porters and hotel staff.

▶ *In this village near San Francisco in the rainforest, many people make their living selling traditional pottery to tourists.*

Information technology (IT)

The information technology industry is a fast-growing sector in Peru. In the past, IT businesses were primarily situated in coastal cities, but now many inland areas are home to computing and communications companies. The effect of technological change in rural areas has been uneven. While some people may still be unfamiliar with the use of a public telephone, others – often the younger generation – are becoming keyboard literate.

◄ *Despite the information technology boom, these professional letter-writers are still kept busy by those Peruvians who cannot afford a typewriter, let alone a computer.*

In response to the rapid growth in IT, schools and training centres are acquiring computers and introducing information technology courses. Computer technology is quickly becoming an important part of the way Peruvians communicate with each other and with people in other countries. As in many countries throughout the world, new technology is bringing a greater sense of being part of a global community. The internet revolution has also increased pressure on people to learn English, as it is the language of the most readily available computer programs. Consequently, English language courses are also becoming much more widely available.

◄ *An invitation to come and join the information technology revolution at a computer centre in Lima.*

The growth in IT services has changed the face of the Peruvian workforce. As well as jobs in the design, manufacture and maintenance of computer and communication products, positions in teaching, website design and retail have opened up as a direct result of the demand for new technologies. Most businesses in Peru now rely on computers in order to run smoothly.

IN THEIR OWN WORDS

'My name is Jose Luís Ortiz Velasco. I am 25. I studied economics and now I own and run an internet café. My dream is to run a big business and be part of the global economy. Four years ago internet cafés started to appear and now there is a lot of competition. The charges are very low – 60 cents an hour. Now a lot of schools are teaching computer studies but they don't have very good resources and find it difficult to get good teachers. I learnt by myself and found out how to build, repair and configure computers.'

9

The Way Ahead

It is nearly 500 years since a Spaniard experiencing Peru and its people for the first time wrote: 'The time has come to take my pen in hand and report the great things there are to tell of Peru...'

The beginning of the twenty-first century saw Peru return to a democratically elected government after a period of political and social instability. While there are still great things to tell of Peru, the new government and the people of Peru also have many challenges to overcome. Severe air pollution, poor waste disposal and overcrowding are just some of the environmental hazards in Peru's cities. Meanwhile, logging, soil erosion and water pollution are threatening the spectacular plant and animal life in the Andes and Amazon regions. There are still major inequalities in wealth and standards of living across Peru, with over a quarter of Peruvians living in extreme poverty.

▼ *This modern mural in Cusco shows the Peruvian people's struggle for justice. The return to democracy has meant that human rights and justice all are high priorities for the Peruvian government.*

Yet Peruvians have many reasons to be optimistic about their future. Health and educational opportunities are constantly improving, and Peruvians are working hard to make their cities better places to live. Many people who moved from rural areas to the cities in the late twentieth century in order to escape terrorism have been able to return to the countryside. There is now access by road and plane to many remote areas of the mountains and rainforest and in these regions local people are benefiting from increased trade and tourism.

◀ *This girl in Lima looks forward to a happy future.*

IN THEIR OWN WORDS

'My name is Juan Carlos Puma Chuctaya. I'm 21 and a student studying to pass the exam to enter university to do electrical engineering. I'm also working as a taxi driver twelve hours a day to earn enough to pay for the course. I have to hire a taxi and often I only just make enough to pay for it. I like the traditions of Peru. I like the possibilities for adventure that there are in my country, the myths we have and the mysterious side to our culture. My dream is to study and to get a profession. I would like to study abroad. I want to study technology because I want to be part of the future of this country.'

Glossary

Agriculture Farming the land to produce food.

Apus Traditional spirit gods of the Incas, linked with mountains.

Archaeological Ancient remains of buildings, objects or people that tell us about the way people lived in the past.

Autocratic A system of government in which one powerful person or small group makes all the decisions about the running of the country.

Ayni Inca custom of co-operative work and exchange.

Bismuth A metal used in various ways, including the production of plastic toys and cosmetics.

Campesinos Peasant farmers.

Cloud forest Forest high up on mountain slopes.

Conquistadores The sixteenth-century Spanish conquerors of South America.

Constitution The laws that set out how a country's government is run.

Convention An international document that binds a group of countries in an agreement.

Co-operative Group of people sharing ownership and profits of a farm, company or business.

Costa Coastal region.

Criollo Person of mixed-race parents.

Deforestation Cutting down trees for timber or firewood.

Democratic A system of government in which the population votes for its leaders.

Economy All the business activity in a country.

Ecosystem A community of different plants and animals and the environment they live in.

Eco-tourism Tourism that damages the natural environment and local cultures as little as possible.

Episodes A closely connected series of events.

Erosion The slow disappearance of topsoil from land by water or wind.

Export To sell goods to other countries.

Fertilizer A substance added to the soil to help plants to grow.

Gross National Product The value of all goods and services produced by a country during a certain period.

Hydroelectricity Energy produced by water power, as when rivers are dammed to drive generators.

Import To buy goods from other countries.

Indigenous Descendants of the oldest-known people of an area.

Life expectancy The average number of years people in a particular region or country are expected to live.

Mangrove A forest growing in swamp areas.

Mestizo Mixed-race.

Microclimate A small area that has a different climate from the region around it.

Mineral A naturally occurring rock, such as coal.

Mysticism A belief that spiritual truth can be reached through visions and intuition.

Plankton Microscopic life forms in the seas that are a natural source of food for fish.

Population The total number of people in a place at a given time.

Quechua One of the languages of the Incas, widely spoken in Peru today. Also a group of indigenous people in Peru.

Reforestation Planting new trees to replace those that have been cut down.

Repression When the government prevents people from exercising their rights or expressing certain opinions.

Rural Relating to the countryside.

Shaman A traditional healer.

Sierra Mountain region.

Selva Rainforest region.

Subsistence agriculture Farming in which most of the produce is consumed by the farmer with little left over for sale.

Terrorism Using violence to achieve political aims.

Tropical A very hot, wet climate that occurs in the region between the Tropics of Cancer and Capricorn.

Urban A built-up area, such as a town or a city.

Further Information

Books

Eyewitness: Aztec, Inca and Maya
(Dorling Kindersley, 2005)

Peru: Cultures of the World (2nd Ed) by Kieran Falconer (Benchmark Books, 2006)

Peru: the Land (The Lands, Peoples and Cultures) by Bobbie Kelman and David Schimpky (Crabtree Publishing, 1994)

Peru: the People and Culture (The Lands, Peoples and Cultures) by Bobbie Kelman and Tammy Everts (Crabtree Publishing, 1994)

Websites

http://www.perulinks.com
A webpage that provides links to hundreds of sites about Peru, from education and entertainment to government and politics.

http://www.limapost.com
The daily newspaper of Lima, Peru's capital, in English.

http://www.virtualperu.net
This website features information about Peru's geography and history, as well as photographs of its stunning landscape.

http://www.mountainvoices.org
A website presenting interviews with over 300 people who live in mountain and highland regions around the world, including Peru.

Useful addresses

Peruvian Embassy and Consulate
in the United Kingdom
52 Sloane Street
London SW1X 9SP
Tel: 020 7235 7917
Website: www.peruembassy-uk.com
Email: postmaster@peruembassy-uk.com

Anglo-Peruvian Society
P.O. Box 494
Wembley HA9 8ZB
The Anglo-Peruvian Society is a charity that aims to inform British people about the people, history, language and culture of Peru, and relieve poverty amongst Peruvians.

Peru Support Group
c/o CIIR, Unit 3
Canonbury Yard
190a New North Road
London N1 7BJ
Tel: 020 7354 9825
Website: http://www.perusupportgroup.org.uk
This organization aims to increase public awareness of Peru in Britain and support the people of Peru, especially in the area of human rights.

Index

Numbers in **bold** are pages where there is a photograph or illustration.